Marketing Hotels & Tourism Online

WEBSITE

Make your website engage, convert and get more direct bookings

Ian R. Clayton

EasyAsApplePieBooks.com

Marketing Hotels & Tourism Online

This book is based off of the author's earlier book "How to Build Your Business Online" and has been rewritten specifically for the hotel and tourism industry. It has been updated to reflect the latest successful strategies in marketing.

Foreword & Praise for This Book

This is a 'must-read' for any hotel and tourism manager or owner. Over several months, we embarked on a video marketing and social media campaign using the strategies outlined here. In that time we were ranked on top of results for our target keywords on all search engines. We were the only resort in our category listed on the first page of Google at a time when not even our Tourism Authority Site was listed.

You will find this book easy to read and quickly understand how the strategies and tactics can build your brand and direct business.

Margaux Daher, Poinsettia Apartments, St. Lucia.

In these pages you'll find hope – hope that your tourism business can thrive even now, in an environment of abundant change. Renewed hope that you can get back to what attracted you to hospitality in the first place rather than spending too much time putting out fires and trying to get new customers. Most importantly, it provides a process for helping you connect with the right people who really will appreciate what it is that you offer.

Ian explains Internet Marketing and the new media landscape in a simple, conversational style that makes for an easy read. That's not to say any of this complicated strategy was over-simplified. In fact, I'm delighted to see how elegantly Ian navigates through some of the deepest thinking on marketing and how he sums up what is happening with search and the internet in general. His views on the future of travel are profound yet so well explained that you grasp it in a second.

Any Tourism professional wanting to master online marketing to increase their direct bookings should read and re-read this book. It can literally turn a business around.

Thanks Ian. Through your book, you're making a difference.

Mike Koenigs, CEO, Mixiv

Preface

Are OTAs Eating your Apples?

Yes, I know that it is a bit provocative but a respected editor put me up to it. It is the subtitle of the 3rd book in this series. He suggested that it should the title for the entire series because it is provocative and it touches on one of the major problems with tourism marketing today -. the growing power of OTAs at the expense of the hotel brands and direct bookings.

I have compromised by adding it here in the preface to the first in the series.

OTAs are a vital part of the marketing mix but over the past few years, they have grown to the point where they now approaching parity with direct booking on hotel websites. For small hotels, the ratio is as high as 75% for OTAs to 25% for the Brand.

That may seem grand but it comes at a cost. It is not just commissions; what is most important is the loss of brand integrity and control. Hotels run the risk of becoming a commodity. It started to happen to the airlines but they were big enough to fight back, which they did by drastically reducing and, in some cases, eliminating commission on seat sales.

Owners of independent Hotels do not have that power, but as owners, managers and marketers, we can all be doing a lot more to get our message out and be more engaged in marketing using digital media (book 2) and taking advantage of the technology (book 3) that levels the playing field.

This book - the first in the series - is about your message and your website. It is not about design but about strategy. About how to build and prefect your web presence and messaging to influence and succeed in digital marketing and win back presence in a market that is in danger of shifting away from your control.

Why Apples?

The apple has represented knowledge from as far back in history as the story of Adam and Eve. A falling apple led Sir Isaac Newton to discover gravity. It is famously used as the Logo for the company that thinks differently and also built the first personal computer.

I use it because, to me, it represents discovery, learning and simplicity. Apples are simple to understand and they are good for you. My aim is to make this book easy to understand. I hope you will find it as easy as apple pie.

Now, I don't expect you as hotel manger and tourism operator to do all the work outlined here: Rather it is a guide to what you may get a marketing professional to do. It will help you understand what it needed and be in a better position to select the right professionals and evaluate their work.

On the book covers, the world map is etched in the Apple. This is a fitting metaphor for travel - to learn and discover different cultures and lifestyles, to get away and restore our senses.

It is one of the largest and fastest growing industries in the world. It is the largest service sector industry in the world, employing a huge force of dedicated men and women who offer us hospitality and experiences worth living for.

And like the Apple, travel is good for us; it nourishes the mind and spirit.

Table of Contents

Introduction

Dear Friend,

First, thanks to you for taking the time and making the effort to check out my book is in order. In all likelihood, we come from the same industry - hospitality and tourism - and we both know how busy this industry can be and how difficult it is to make the commitment to check out new ideas and methods, ESPECIALLY when you are already up to your ears in work.

The good news is that I can almost guarantee you that, by the time you're done with this book, you are going to be returning the 'thank you' in my direction. Because the information you are going to learn will change the way you market and its effectiveness. You will start building real authority, get better position and visibility in your market and get more direct bookings to increase your profit line and your return on investment. That is, as long as you approach what you're about to learn with an open mind and are willing to take action.

After all, no method will work unless you work it.

More good news: This book is certainly directed to those working in the tourism and hospitality industry; however the principles, tips and advice given could benefit a wide range of businesses.

So if you're working in another area you're still in luck.

Learning how to use the internet and online media to build your brand has universal applications. This is the future of business and the future is now.

If you aren't learning how to master these elements of business, this is a good time to start because your competition will not be standing still. You're about to learn techniques that will re-define your concept of what marketing is. Not understanding what needs to be done in the new digital world versus doing it right could be the difference between failure and success.

Just watch.

Who am I and how am I qualified to teach you the "ins and outs" of building your brand on the internet?

Good question.

My name is Ian R. Clayton and I'm not only the CEO of a tourism development company, but I'm also an expert in technology and marketing. I've used this unique skill set to not only build my successful tourism business ventures, but also to help position, market and promote several tourism brands, using the exact strategies and techniques I'm about to share with you.

Your success depends on a combination of knowledge, experience, resources and hard work. All of this can be outsourced today; you simple have to know what, how and who. The 'what' and 'how' are covered in this book at a strategic level. In the next in the series, I will share more on the tactics, resources and who you may use to help implement and manage ongoing campaigns.

This book is not another theoretical study by someone who will tell you what you need to do and has never done it. All the strategies and tactics are tried and test. I've used (and am still using) the exact methods that we'll be going over together.

Are you ready to learn the techniques of marketing hospitality and tourism online and using the internet and social media to build your brand?

Good. Because the adventure is about to begin.

Sincerely,

Ian

Get Next eBook @99c

Register to Get Free Bonuses, training videos and resources: This will also register you for the Pre-launch of the next book in the series. I will invite you, by email, to get the next book at just 99c when it is pre-launched on Amazon.

http://Bonus.MarketingHotelsTourismOnline.com

Travel Marketing Then and Now

Hospitality, hotel management and tourism make up a lifestyle, and not simply an occupation. For many small hotel owners, it is long hours and on-call duty 24/7. Hoteliers must be a Jack & Jill of all trades. Daytimes spent looking after guests, checking on staff and covering details of housekeeping, the gardens, the pool, the bar and restaurants. We continually put out fires in all areas: catering to others, dealing with problems, fixing pool pumps, organising maintenance and repairs, painting and sometimes even serving at the bar when we have to.

As owner/manager of a small hotel, a restaurant, bar, a catamaran sailing cruise operation, a safari tour or any small tourism activity and attraction the most rewarding times are often when you are doing it all yourself, particularly when your guests show their appreciation for what you do for them.

The larger tourism companies, hotels and resorts have managers and others to delegate to, but even then running the enterprise is a full time job.

It's a continuous stream of work, keeping all things up to standard and adding appropriate services that you know are needed to keep your guests happy and enjoying the experience sufficiently enough to return again.

Then there is all that accounting, billing, reporting and systems that we need today: Food and beverage systems, payroll, housekeeping, property management systems, reservations and marketing.

It's a bit complicated at times and is getting more so with all the changes that are happening. It requires a good deal of knowledge and expertise.

ON TOP OF ALL THAT ... People are now telling you that you must be doing more brand marketing; you need a mobile website for every smartphone, a social media plan and you simple have to do more online marketing, as that is where all media is moving.

Yet ANOTHER set of things to learn ... Along with your already 'full-time' job ... When exactly are you supposed to do this? In your spare time? Phew, that looks like a pile of stress!

Marketing has changed

It used to be that we built a hotel, attended trade shows got a rep, gave inventory to a tour operator, hired a PR firm, listed with the tourism authority and looked after guests. That was it. Agents, Tour Operators, Tourism Associations and reps have all changed and we now face a different set of rules and demands. Distribution has become a very costly game and, as a result, the new tour operators don't even want to deal with small properties. To a very worrying extent, the tourism product, hotel rooms and activities, have become commodities easily substitutable and widely discounted.

In fact, the entire marketing and advertising world has turned upside down and is still changing as we speak.

We are experiencing the greatest rate of change and innovation in information technology, systems networking, publishing and marketing in the history of the world. In his ground-breaking book, "Abundance", Peter Diamandis documents the exponential rate of change in several key sectors, particularly in communications. As he puts it, we are now all participants in the World Wide Web of instantaneous, low-cost communications and information abundance.

Almost everyone can create, publish, distribute and promote blogs, articles, videos, magazines and books. The tools to do this are available at a fraction of the cost they were just a few years ago, when they were used only by the privileged few. Today they are embedded in smartphone applications, platforms and networks that are often freely available.

As the world has moved to embrace more decentralised and automated communications, traditional publishers and broadcasters have seen their once organised world become mayhem. The internet and online media has forced them to adapt and change, as well.

The new media is a decentralised network that ties people together. It has become a highly intelligent system, with automated processes that can dispatch, decipher and coordinate all communications and information instantly.

Marketing in the Age of Participation

You do not, of course, have to participate but, if you don't, you will be left behind. Businesses are telling their stories and sharing more with clients, in more personal ways, than ever before. It's not just something they're compelled to do; it's something they're *expected* to do.

As hotel managers, tourism and hospitality professionals, we can and must engage with the new media and tell our own story. In this age of abundance, there are things we can and must do in order to stand out. This book is about those mastering the new media and making it work for you. Even if you choose to outsource it all, the concepts outlined in this book will help guide you in selecting the right partners and keeping them on track.

But Relax ... That's why I wrote this book for you.

I've been in the hospitality business for years, trained with one of the largest hotel and catering chains in Europe, managed restaurants, been a chef, a caterer, a receptionist, barman, head waiter and hotel manager ... I left it to study systems and marketing at university. I went onto study Computer Science at a Master's level.

I started my company, AXSES, in 1984, offering systems advice and solutions to small business, and in 1990 won a competition for innovation that got me back into the tourism industry. With a grant from the Canadian government, we pioneered mapping and marketing systems for tourism and went into production with the Barbados Tourism Authority.

Like many things in life, the plan was a stepping stone pathway with a few stones missing and a meandering route. In the end, we built a hugely successful website and marketing platform for tourism. That was the Barbados Tourism Encyclopaedia: http://barbados.org. 20 years later, it is still the most popular and most linked site on Barbados anywhere, even in the face of the government spending million of dollars promoting their own site.

Along the way, we have helped many companies build powerful information systems and market their brand to bring in more direct bookings.

Now, I have written all this down in simple, easy-to-understand terms. You want to know how to get the most out of the online media, how to build your brand, get more done with fewer resources, make more profit and live the life you deserve.

THIS is "THAT" Book Series...

By reading this book series, you will learn enough to know that there are lots of ways to improve your marketing. You will also learn that you can mess up and that there are some people who will take all your money for "marketing" you online and deliver you squat.

Hopefully, this series will keep you far away from making these mistakes.

Your Tourism Marketing Plan

Of course, we all know that it is important to have a plan as you start anything. Well, that gets hard to create if you don't really understand what you need to do. This can be really frustrating and bewildering. Luckily for you, we will cover all you need to know to create a workable plan. This chapter will guide you through the mindset of making your plan. In reality, this book series *is* your plan.

When you have completed the series, you will realize that it is structured in the very steps that you need to follow in order to start marketing your business. All you need to do is follow it in the sequence that it is front of you. That really is your plan. It outlines what you need to do in very simple, easy-to-follow steps.

Your plan doesn't need to be set in stone or in complete detail, but it does need to have a target that you want to reach—otherwise, how will you know when you've got there? Think of your marketing plan as a battle plan. Your company's profitability in the future is at stake, along with the joy of running your hotel or tourism business.

But what's your end goal? You want more loyal guests and better customers. You want customers that are happy with their holidays with you and will recommend your hotel or service to others. Is that really asking too much?

Not at all! In fact, that is an important part of the plan that often gets overlooked. You want your guests to be your ambassadors. You want them to write reviews on TripAdvisor and tell their friends about your place.

There are several things you must do for this to happen, beyond being the best host of a wonderful experience. You need a social media campaign and a continuity program. Both of these are discussed in the chapter on your sales funnel and more details on implementation will be covered later in the series.

Be the "Go-to Place" for your niche

You want to become the "must-visit place" for your particular niche, and more likely than not, you will have several niches: Who is your prime target? Is it adventure travellers, families, romance, getaways, beach holidays?

In a lot of cases, it will be many of these because these are topics and not real markets. A lot of your competitors may be advertising and listing in the family holidays category, and if that is exactly who you want to cater to, you need to drill down and define the personalities within that group that you want to cater to. Are they wealthy and sophisticated or the more budget-conscious, rustic types?

Personalisation makes the difference

In one of our projects, called RealHolidays, we defined hotels and guests around personality types. The system tracked travellers' clicks and preferences and created a personality profile based on these triggers. We matched travellers to hotels with similar profiles based on these psychological triggers. This technique is not applied in hospitality much, but it has great potential.

The triggers and the technique are explained in the FREE BONUS package for book buyers. You will find a link to the bonus at the end of this book.

Travellers, like any shopper, want to work with the people they trust, know and like. They want a host or guide who is an expert and that offers a great experience. Today's travellers are looking for an experience they can call their own. If you can define who your ideal customer is and create an environment just for them, you will be on your way to offering holidays that are exclusively theirs.

Holidays.exclusivelyours.com is a project in the works right now and it is built using advanced matching and profiling techniques. You can start thinking like this now and plan to offer tailor-made holidays based on personality. We will go into that in detail in the next book.

Reputation matters

When a traveller is shopping for places to stay and things to do, they are comparing your hotel or product with everyone else and nearly all of them are looking at reviews. Reputation is one of the most important criteria when choosing a place to stay, eat or play. Over 90% of shoppers look at reviews, and they look at 6-10 reviews on average before they book. You will absolutely have to have a reputation management system in place. It can be fancy or something you do yourself. We will look into this in more detail later in the book.

Hospitality matters

Another deciding factor is who the host is. That is why so many people check out the online travel agents and still book direct with the hotel. They compare prices and features and 50% still go direct to meet and chat with the hotel manager. Personality matters and travellers like to be with like-minded people.

Personality and authenticity is a huge factor in choosing a hotel, guest house, inn, an apartment accommodation or a resort. It's a principle foundation of everything you need to do online for your brand. This is one of the reasons why we encourage owners to be featured in their videos. It creates celebrity to some extent but most of all, it creates authenticity.

Celebrity works wonders. Richard Branson knows that, but not everyone will fly balloons or scale buildings. Celebrity can be much more modest and you can become the expert in your niche by offering exceptional services to help travellers shop.

Did you get that? Help Travellers Shop!

Yes, we all do it to some extent, and all the big boys pay a lot of attention to providing travellers with shopping tools. But it's not done very effectively in travel and hardly at all by smaller independent hotels and tourism companies. I will show you why later but, for now, just keep it in mind as you read on because it is one of the most misunderstood parts of travel marketing.

Now let's get back to your magnetic positioning and your brand. To be truly magnetic, it helps to be different, original and rare. Being mysterious, exciting and exclusive will create intrinsic value that will totally separate you for the crowd. Cultivate intrinsic value in your service and your product to win lasting customers who become your advocates. Provide intrinsic value way before they are ready to buy and you will grab their attention long before others do.

There it is again – Help them shop. – Could you think of something you can give your prospective clients as they start shopping that will help them sort out the options and make a decision? Travellers look at over two dozen sites and rarely book on first encounter; so you have to give them a reason to return. It's an advanced concept which we will discuss further in the next issue of this book. But keep it in mind, as it is all part of building the perfect sales funnel.

Offering the best service and best product is not enough today, you need to be seen and heard. And if you really understand your guests, you can offer them something that most others miss.

So, now it's time to get to work. First, I'll help you understand how it all works in the online world right now.

How online travel works

Let's use an example of looking for family hotels in your destination *[we use Barbados in our example]*. You instantly use the computer for your initial search.

Travellers have many options; they can go to Online Travel Agents (OTAs) like Booking.com, TripAdvisor and their favourite social network, like Pinterest or Facebook. There are new travel sites popping up all over the place, but Search is one of the first ports of call. Imagine if you are looking for a place to stay. Google is probably the first place you might start— it is the starting point for many travel shoppers and it is the most popular search engine. But you could use Yahoo, Bing or others!

Start by typing what you are looking for in the search engine - "family holidays in *Barbados*", for example. This is a keyword phrase which, most of the time, will return a list of big brands, review sites and Online Travel Agents (OTAs).

The top of the list is usually full of sponsored results. These are ads and they're at the top simply because people have paid for them to be there. Once the advertiser stops paying, they will be removed from the top. You'll see this with all different types of searches.

Just to let you know, the ads are created through a programme called AdWords. It is an advertising model, using Pay-Per-Click (PPC). You choose your keywords, bid on a space and pay whenever your ad is clicked on. This isn't always the best route, unless you have an unlimited marketing budget or have experience in this type of marketing. Without experience, you could soon see your budget diminishing but no results from it.

Scroll down to get past the ads and then you'll get to the organic results. Most of the time, you will find 10 results per page. They can be a mixture of videos, articles, blogs and websites that Google (or your search engine) deems RELEVANT to your search.

It's really important to remember the word RELEVANT. Google is interested in relevancy. Think about it: if you're looking for family hotels in *[your destination]*, but gained results from oatmeal cookie recipes to how to sharpen a pencil, you'd never bother with Google again. Google would lose revenue, respect and users and that isn't something the search engine giant wants to happen! So, it's important that all results are relevant to the searcher.

Keeping that in mind, Google will want to show your business if it thinks it will be relevant for a user's search. But that isn't all it uses to determine rankings. Google wants authority sites to make sure that their business is meaningful and run by professionals.

Let's go to a specific example, that of searching for "family hotels in Barbados". You'll see there are 63 million results Google believes to be relevant and right for you. Does that mean you're going to go through each of them?

Definitely not!

Chances are you'll stop looking once you've finished looking at the first page. If you do go further, you're not likely to go past the first couple of pages. Could you imagine going through all those pages? Most people stop searching from the first set of organic results. They believe those are the best ones—the ones, in old print newspaper terms, that are "above the fold". They're the ones on the first page of the newspaper; the reason for someone to buy it! When it comes to online, they are those that you can see without having to scroll.

The results at the top usually receive more clicks than those at the bottom.

Without jumping too far ahead in this book, you want to be AT THE TOP! You want to get as high up on the list as possible and that's something your competitors are after.

Don't try to trick the search engine. This is something Google HATES with a passion. There are many companies and freelancers out there who will use *black hat SEO* techniques but they are the type that will get you ranking high under false pretences. While the tactics do keep changing, Google does figure them out and the websites using them eventually get banned.

So, how can you convince Google your stuff is good?

Offer content that's real and valuable to your readers. Don't get pulled into the games of SEO.

Really, it's similar to a popularity contest. Someone uses search terms and then Google will look all over the internet for the best results. It will look at your site—if it's good enough to catch the attention of the robots—and determine whether the information is relevant. It then looks at other websites and determines how relevant your website is compared to them. Those who already have the respect of Google will get special attention. You want to tick all the right boxes so your site and respected sites online are all voting for you.

The other part of Planning is what we call the "Game Plan". As you read this book, think of it as steps in your marketing plan. You will need to start thinking about what sort of time and resources you will need, what budget you will allocate, what work you will do yourself, what you will outsource and who you might outsource to.

Throughout the rest of this book and the others that follow, I'll share with you the essential things you must have in your plan to achieve a successful online brand.

Your future success is going to be your brand. Building your brand will be the focus of the plan that this series will help you define and develop. The OTAs have a brand, and you must too. No matter how small you are, it is brands that matter today in search and marketing, both online and offline.

Branding is the name of the game in just about every market. Companies that have managed to get products on shelves by relying on distribution channels are realising that they have to become marketing companies and build a brand that resonates with consumers. A major retailer recently told a longtime supplier: "What I want from you is a brand, and that means you have to get good at marketing. If I want a product, I'll make it myself."

In travel, hotels and tourism suppliers face that dilemma with OTAs. Without a brand, you are a commodity and an OTA will switch the client to where they want. We know they do that and we will show you the proof in this series. But with a brand, they can be your best advocates. With a brand, you gain more control over distribution and that can build more direct bookings.

To build your brand, you first must define your niche, your mission, your special personality and your difference. Then you need to build your authority, trust and get noticed on the internet. The rest of the plan is just a matter of helping people find the thing that they need and want—you!

The Keys to Traffic

With most marketing projects, you need to go through a phase of preparation. It's tedious, boring and tricky but it is crucial if you want success.

This is that preparation phase.

Skip this and you will get to move on to the fun parts and play with all the cool gadgets. But you'll certainly struggle to use them correctly. Think of it like climbing a ladder—sure, you're on there but are you going to the right window?

But what is this preparation stage? It's the keyword research.

Yes, it's boring and it can be technical but you need it. Without it, there's no point going ahead because you won't get the best results.

Knowing how annoying this is, we want to make it as easy as possible.

What Is Keyword Research?

People use keywords for finding information, services and products in Google (and other search engines!). It could be one single word or a whole phrase—usually a few words in length. You may have heard that keywords are dead but that is simply not true. What is true is that other things have become more important and you can't overstuff your content with keywords. In fact, you have to be very careful how you use them, but they are still a vital part of your marketing.

Keyword research is studying what people are looking for and how they use the keywords in their search. It seems so straightforward at first but then you go deeper into it. Let's go back to our family holidays in *your destination* example. When you do the research, you may find that people use the following words to find the same information:

- Family Hotels in *your destination*

- Children-Friendly Hotels in *your destination*

- Hotels with Kids Clubs in *your destination*

- *Your destination* Family holidays

- *Your destination* Family vacations

- *Your destination* Hotels where kids are free

- *Your destination* Hotels with babysitting

- …and many other varieties

People can often search in the strangest of ways—and often in ways that you would not usually imagine. They can search with slang, misspellings, poor grammar, 'wrong' terms, specifics and generalities that are simply mind-boggling to say the least!

You simply cannot predict how customers will search for you online. Don't even try—chances are you will be wrong without even knowing it!

Most people fall into the following four traps when doing their keyword research:

Trap #1: Skipping It

You now know that this is just something you shouldn't do!

Trap #2: Looking at Your Competitor's Website

You want to do this stage quickly, right? Well, isn't copying from your competitor the best way to get ahead? This is just like copying off your friend's school paper—it isn't necessarily going to be the right answer. Just because a competitor is using a certain phrase doesn't mean it is the best one for you!

Do you really know how your competitor found the words? Do you even know if they're converting well? It's already hard enough to get Google to 'like' you; it will be even harder when it's with bad phrases. What's even worse is that you're competing directly with someone else in the market!

Trap #3: Forgetting to Use the Keywords You Find

So, after compiling that long list of great words and phrases to use, they get filed away for when the time comes to create the content. Great! Except that most people forget to go back to that list and use the keywords they find! Think of it like buying custom-crafted marble tiles but opting for inexpensive laminate ones when it comes to redecorating your kitchen.

You need to check over your list once you've got your keywords to make sure your marketing works.

Trap #4: Only Doing the Keyword Research Once

Keyword research isn't a one-time thing; it's ongoing. You can't just cross it off your list once you've done it and never do it again. Why not? Well, there are a few important reasons.

There are many ways that people will find your website. That offers you many options to use with your keywords. You can't go after them all at once, though.

Instead of doing all the research at once, it's best to do it on one particular area, such as family holidays, and then focus on a different area at a later date. It can be easy to find yourself trapped in the research stage.

Your products or services are not set in stone. They are always changing, which means you'll need to do keyword research again in the future. You may add a spa treatment and want to market that. That means you need to find out the keywords that people use to find that type of treatment and exactly what kind of treatment they are looking for on their holiday. As your business offers or conditions change, you'll need to make sure your presence online changes as well.

How Keyword Research Works

You can do this in a few ways but none of them are easy and quick! There are some that will help you to simplify the situation, though. Just make sure you allow yourself hours (several of them) to get this process done.

There are some keyword research tools that you have to pay for—some one-time and others on a monthly basis—but there are free options. There are some that are really simple to use but others may not be appropriate due to the steep learning curve.

It is possible to hire someone and outsource this stage; there are plenty of experts about. They will already be using the best tools on the market and know how to use them all effectively. Buying these great tools isn't worthwhile if you're using them in snippets. By the time you come back to using them, you'll have forgotten how they worked!

Selecting the Right Keywords

It's easy to make the mistake of thinking that your product is the keyword. For example, a submarine expedition over the coral reefs is an activity that many people will enjoy, but few will think of searching for a submarine trip or excursion. In this case you need to market to people who like to snorkel or enjoy diving to see the beautiful coral reefs and tropical fish.

Few people going on holiday have ever thought of searching for a submarine trip, cruise or excursion. Your market is actually not people looking for submarines at all. It's people who search for snorkelling, diving and many who have never thought of searching for either. Your market is also all of those who can't swim or are afraid of the water and would love to see the corals and the reef fish from the comfort of a port seat in a dry submersible vehicle that is safe and secure. We will delve into this later in the section, "When Keywords Fail You!" in the following book in this series.

Keyword Tools

All that being said, there are some keyword tools worth considering. These include:

Google's Keyword Tool

Google Keyword Tool is connected to the AdWords advertising program, and with its recent changes, you will need to log in to your Goggle account to use this tool. You don't have to run ads in order to use it. You will be able to see how well keywords compete with Google's paid advertisers and how many people are searching for certain words. Now, this is not always going to be available but it is one of the best tools and it is well worth working with for as long as we can. Once you log in into adwords.google.com, click on the 'Keyword Planner" at the top of the page.

There are two primary ways to use this tool. The **first method** is what Google current calls "**search for new keywords using a phrase, website or category**". You select that option and just enter some seed words (ideas) into the search box. You could also enter your website address into the website field so Google can guess the topic of your website. If you like, you can also select a category from a list that Google will give you.

Using the tool by entering seed words will help Google find relevant suggestions. You may be surprised by some of the options that come up. You'll find that words are misspelled—searchers don't know or really care about typing words correctly—or there may be incorrect terms as people try to use jargon or semantics.

You may find terms that are far more specific or vague than you considered. Searches for "air conditioning" could come up with specific part numbers or company names. For the most part, the suggestions are usually quite good but there will often be some that are off your topic completely.

If you already have a good idea and don't need the suggestion, you can use the **second method** and just enter a list of possible keywords using the "**Find new keywords and get search volume data**" option.

In either case, the information that you need to look at is the amount of people searching for specific keyword phrases during the month. Google and YouTube are full of tutorials to help you learn more about gathering and interpreting the data. There are also other ways to research the words to give you much more or even less valuable information.

You will see measures of competitiveness and the amount people are paying for ads to appear when the words are searched. It also tells you how many people are searching for those words. Remember, this is a tool for advertisers!

How Google Ranks Keywords

Today, search engines like Google are checking your site to find what your **Content Keywords are** and what they mean in the context of the entire site. Google Webmaster Tools will list your site's keywords according to how often they are found on your site's pages. They don't actually rank Exact Match Keywords (EMKs) at all, just single words. Regardless of the rank, searchers will type in exact phrases, so EMKs are important. Ranking is now all about how keywords are scattered on your pages and what they mean in the context of other words. Words that have similar and complementary meanings reinforce the message of your pages. For this reason, it is import to write content that has supporting words and words that expand the subject, giving it depth.

Deeper Meaning

Yes, it is a bit academic-sounding, I know. Just imagine you want your page to be significant for families who are looking for a holiday. You address that with content about the feature and benefits of your hotel or destination. Now, search will check the page and index the words looking for meaning and check for depth. If it finds "family holidays" a whole lot of times, it will not see that as very deep. You need to write about children, kids' activities, kids clubs, seniors, and specific things that families of all ages can do.

If you understand the problem of seniors, for example, and show concern and insight like, "the beach is smooth, sloping gradually into the water, making it safe and fun for even the more elderly family members to enjoy floating in ocean" your page will be better understood.

Got it? See how that sentence touches on a real understanding of emotions and feelings in the experience, and see how those words "smooth beach", "sloping... into the water", "safe", "fun", "ocean" and "floating" convey meaning with deeper significance than just "family holidays".

Market Samurai

This is one of the tools that you need to pay for but it isn't going to set the budget back too much. It's very robust and doesn't just give you suggestions. There are multiple filters so your suggestions are more applicable to your website. Some of the data is taken from the Google reports.

Search volume and keyword suggestions aren't the only information you get. You will be able to see the top 10 competitors in your industry for particular keywords. You can gain valuable information about the marketing efforts of these companies to help you surpass them.

It will also help you track the progress of your website as you dominate the internet. You can see how well your site ranks on Yahoo, Bing and Google for the keywords you use. The information displays the page that shows up with the keywords, whether you're losing any ground (or gaining any!), the number of pages indexed—viewed by the search engines—and number of backlinks (something we'll cover later in the book) going to your website.

Market Samurai also helps you find articles, videos and quotes that can help you in creating and enhancing your own content. It is full of features and functions. There are plenty of video tutorials created by the publisher and on YouTube. Learning this software is possible and much easier than many others.

Hittail

This is another paid-for tool that does far more than list keywords. It needs to be integrated with your Google Webmaster Tools and once that is done, Hittail will access all the data on visitors and keywords and analyse which keywords are the best for you. It will tell you which phrases you should target based on your existing traffic. It uses a sophisticated process that is fine-tuned by analyzing over 1.2 billion keywords.

Other Tools

If you like to experiment and know just what's available, then check out some of these other tools. The professional SEO people will use several, as they all have their own specialty.

Keywordeye.com gives you a great visual display, showing the most popular word in **LARGE** letters and sizing down to the least popular. In addition, the colour of the most competitive words and the least differ, which makes it really easy to pick and choose based on traffic and competition.

PageRankChecker.com is a tool that lets you look up information on how you and your competitors are ranking with Google (their Page Rank), their links and their most used keywords (density of keywords) and social signals;

all important factors in knowing how you stand relative to others.

KeywordSpy.com will tell you what your competition is doing in advertising. What they are spending, what keywords they are using and even how many clicks they are getting. This is very helpful in knowing their strengths and in stopping opportunities.

Again, I don't suggest that you do this work as it really is very time-consuming and to get the most out of the tools, you do need to subscribe to the paid versions and gain experience in working with them all. The reason I list them is just so you know what is available so that you can check things once in awhile to measure how you are doing.

If you decide that the research is best completed by you, make sure you're ready to spend the time needed - it doesn't matter which software you choose to use. You'll need to learn how to use the tool and then do your research. It isn't fun but you will find that the hours do pay off eventually.

What Is Considered a Good Keyword?

What qualifies as a good keyword? The truth is this depends on geographical area and niche. You generally want to find the words that are the "fruits hanging low". These have low competition but high search numbers. The actual numbers do vary, though.

Eventually, you'll find that sweet spot where the search volume is relatively high but the competition is still low. Focus on these types of words and then look for those with at least similar metrics.

By aiming for highly competitive words, you will find it harder to improve your placement on Google. There are so many other businesses competing with you and they've been doing it for longer! Bigger businesses will have bigger budgets and could even have a dedicated team of Internet marketers. When you find keywords that have low search volumes, there won't be enough people using those phrases to make it worth your while.

Need an example?

Type your name into Google. Chances are you're the first on the list and that makes many people think they're doing great.

You probably do too.

When typing the exact name, your website should come up on top! It should take up most of that first page!

But that doesn't mean your website is doing well. Only those who already know you or have heard about you will find you in this way. It's like having a business card online—they know you exist; they just want to know what you offer.

We're looking for something completely different.

We want people to find you without ever having heard about you in the past. We want them to find you by typing in different terms. The keywords could be the holiday experience you offer, your services, products or even your location.

Ranking for your name is easy! Ranking high for services and products is completely different and not so easy. This is where the online marketing is so important.

By finding that spot where the competition is low but the search volume is high, you're getting there. Save those keywords in a spreadsheet. When using Market Samurai or Google's Keyword Tool, you can quickly export the results straight into a spreadsheet. Google's tool doesn't give you as much information and there is some guesswork afterwards, but it is there!

Now it is time to sort the keyword target list into a priority. You want to know which words or phrases you are targeting first. Colour coding is a great way to do this and to make clear which ones are the most important for you right now. There's no need to focus on more than five or 10 at a time and to move through the list as you see progress.

The next chapter is all about what you do now that you have those keywords that will help your business succeed.

Perfect Your Presence

Τ here's one acronym that you need to know when it comes to your website: SEO. That stands for Search Engine Optimisation and this chapter is about how to make sure your website is seen by the world, using the best SEO practices for getting your site ranked and listed on search results. That has become increasing difficult for small hotels and tourism sites, as Search Engines and particularly Google now favours authority sites like the Online Travel Agents (OTAs) and TripAdvisor. That's why it is vital that you know what to do to get listed.

What Exactly Is SEO?

SEO is a lot about making your website stand out to the search engines. It helps Google realise that your site has all the relevant information for searchers. Each element will do one of two things: repel or appeal to Google.

You need to a site that Google wants to come back to and send people to. If you use tactics that trick, taunt or tease it, it's not going to bother.

The online world revolves around Google—not the other way around!

But what makes Google love a website so much? Like with keyword research, this is just something we don't know all the ins and outs to. We're not sure of everything that Google wants to see but we know some. As a guide, Google wants to recommend a site that a person will stay on. It doesn't want a searcher to go to a site and then quickly click back or visit another site—that makes the bounce rate high. It wants to recommend a site that offers lots of information; all relevant to the searcher.

Remember that your whole aim is to make your website credible. Your visitors need to leave knowing that you know all the answers and are the experts.

Google looks for new sites that have relevant content it looks at old sites to see what has changed. It uses spiders and bots to crawl and index everything on the internet. You want Google to find your site and index it and then keep checking back so more of your pages are found. You do that by building sites that are Search Engine Optimised (SEO).

The Site Your Business Needs

You've probably already got a website for your company—and it's likely to be *BusinessName.com.*.

It can help to have your keyword in your *Business Name*. This was very important just a while ago and it can still help. But search engines are beginning to favour brand names.

Keyword-specific domains are also called **Exact Match Domain Names (EMD).** They got so successful on search results that Google decided to reduce the big bonus an EMD name gets. They did this by paying more attention to the page content and looking for signs of over optimisation. This was to ensure that low-quality sites don't rise high in Google's search results simply because they have search terms in their domain names.

It is not a good idea to use EMD names today as they shout out to Google and other search engines that you are pulling strings. EMD get put under a microscope. My recommendation is DO NOT use an EMD. I still use Partial Matches (PMD) along with a unique qualifier or brand name. This goes for the names you give to domain, your pages and the links within your website as well as the links to your website.

We will cover this in more detail in a future chapter. For now, just remember that your page or site must have quality content and you need to be careful not to overdo the SEO on the page. Just follow the guidelines here to be safe.

What Every Page Needs

Every page is there to offer different content and a different emphasis. However, there are some elements that need to be present so your content is fully optimised.

Now, if you have done the drill down exercise we talked about in the last chapter, this is where you start to get specific and talk to the personality types who make up you market. Make sure your content is relevant in terms of character and tone. Your graphics and design must also be relevant to your visitor. Travellers will leave a site fast if it does not speak to them, so be sure you are using the right words and speaking to the right audience.

The Headline

Compelling headlines are needed on every page of your website. The problem for many website owners is they can't do this. They'll have:

- Welcome!

- ABC Hotel has been Running for X Years

- Come to Us and Forget the Rest

- The Best Little Hotel in XYZ

They just sound boring, right?

Well it is because its all platitudes that everyone uses. So you want to do something different. You want to create headlines that pull people in and communicate just why they should stay at your apartment, inn, villa, hotel or try out your services or products.

You also need to let them know this is the place for them specifically: unpretentious, understated, outlandish or traditional. It has to be tailored to who you want to engage with. One rule is to build for yourself and this way, you will attract like-minded people.

The easy way to do this is focus on the fears and pain that customers have dealt with in the past and how you can make it completely different. People want to escape the pain and suffering that they will love you for trying to help them. Travellers are often afraid of the unknown, how far away is it, is it safe, will I get robed in a taxi on the way. Will it rain everyday? What if I get ill, are there good medical facilities. Can I drink the water. You know the list so put it all in a FAQ page. These are triggers which might become part of he hot-buttons we talk about soon.

While being compelling, you need to make sure your keyword is in there. You need to help people find you in Google—and help Google find you and know that your website will help the searchers.

Keywords

At one time, it was considered good practice to add your keywords everywhere on the site. But that was a long time ago. Google now uses latent semantic indexing to check the language. If yours doesn't flow well or looks unnatural or the same keywords are used over and over again, it won't like you.

The best thing that you can do is take a keyword or phrase and focus on that for each page. You'll then need to add relevant terms into your copy to avoid overusing it but make sure it has that single focus.

There are certain places that you must add your word or phrase:

- The headline

- The sub-headlines

- The first sentence

- In bullet points

- In image tags, alt text, description and in the name of the image file (coming up!)

- Call to actions (coming up!)

- In anchor text (coming up!)

- In list building (you guessed it, coming up too!)

Keyword Density

You also need to pay attention to the keyword density. This is the amount of times your word appears in your content. At one point in time, the higher the density, the better your content was. However, that's no longer the case. There is a simple way to calculate the keyword density of your content:

- Count the number of times the word or phrase is in the content

- Determine the total content word count

- Divide the keyword count by the total count

Luckily, we don't have to do that by hand. There are many free online keyword density calculators that will do that for you, such as: http://kesor.net/keyword-density/

A density between 1% and 2% is what you want to aim for. That means for every 100 words, your word appears between one and two times. Any more than that and it will be hard to make your copy look good and Google is going to start thinking you're spam. You'll ruin your credibility and your content just looks like garbage.

Your Word Count

Google will look at how long your content is to determine if the site is worth indexing. Now, there's no magic number but it is best to have least 400 words on each page. For web pages, it may be better to keep the length under 800 words, as people tend to prefer shorter amounts of text. A good way to present detailed information is to write good headlines followed by a paragraph of overview and then allow readers to click for more info.

The Future of Search

Today's marketers tend to obsess over keyword density, Meta descriptions and link profiles. That is still valid but search engines are becoming intelligent and are looking beyond the word count and obvious tags.

Search engines now incorporate logic and machine learning, involving troves of behavior metrics that gauge the user experience and eveluate a website accordingly. They measure site speed, mobile friendliness, site structure, content, relevance, authority, engagement and many other signals. Ultimately they are looking for websites that provide valid answeres to travelers questions and concerns.

Today you need to think about your website visitors at every stage of your website strategy process. It's all about the users experience, which we delve into, in the next chapter. .

To make your website appear in the Google search results, you have to know what your customers are typing into the search engine. Most might think of terms like "Family Holidays", but search habits have become more semantic and people are now asking whole and complete sentences.

The search term "Family Holidays" has evolved into a far more specific question, such as "what are the best holiday villas in the Caribbean for a family of four at under $250US per night." Further down in the travel shopping cycle, shoppers will be more specific as they look for the "best value villa resorts" in specific islands and areas.

While search has become far more specific, you still have to cover the basic. If you also answer these more specific questions you will be on your way to the top the of search engines. So, ask yourself what your customers need help with and be sure to have those answers on your pages. It's part of the power messaging formula, which we cover in this series.

Formatting

When it comes to reading online, the attention span of your readers is short. Most people won't read every single word that you write so you need to make the content easy to scan and skim. Make it possible for them to pick out the most important parts that they need to read quickly.

Content as one block of text is boring and you'll find people quickly click away. They'll go to your competitors without the competitors doing anything extra! People want to read content that is broken up easily. They want to see the sub-headlines—and it is worth making them bold—so they can easily go through your content. Bullet points are also worth using, as long as you do it conservatively.

White space is a good thing, contrary to popular belief. It makes your pages user-friendly and easy to read. Having a light background with dark text has proven to be the best for reading online. Use something effective, even if light text on a dark background looks better.

Images and Videos

People like to 'see' as well as read about how you can help them. It's a good practice to use images and to name them with the keywords you are targeting. Again, don't overdo this and, if you do use more than one image, make sure you use semantic words and broad terms for all except one. For example, if you are trying to rank in search for "*your destination* beach hotel", use several pictures of the beach and have one named "*yourdestination*-beach-hotel. jpg". Name the other beach, sea or sand image something compatible with words like coastal, swimming, sunbathing, miles of sand etc. Even "Best Island Beach in the Caribbean" is a good general alternative, it reuses the word beach but in a very wide context.

Travellers love videos and research has shown that those who look at a video are far more likely to book. It's not that video will immediately convert a prospect but those who do watch your video will remember it and it will significantly influence their purchase. Travellers who look at video are serious buyers and your video is a powerful marketing tool. Not only that, video keep visits on your site longer and length of stay is one of the factors that Google uses to deterring the ranking of sites.

We will be chatting about how to use videos strategically throughout this book series. The chapter "Hot Buttons and Video" looks at what kind of video you may create, what to say and how to craft your message for maximum impact.

Call to Action

Now that your visitors are on your page and have read what you want them to, it's time to get them to do what you want them to do. Without telling them, they don't know. They may just click away. You need to tell them clearly. It may sound obvious but for most people, it really isn't!

Each website page needs to have a call to action. Tell your visitors what to do next. Many will use your booking engine and you will capture their details to follow up. But many more will not be ready to book. Less than 2% of travellers who visit your site for the first time will book. That means that 98% will leave and maybe go elsewhere. You need to give them other options and reasons to contact you, to request brochures, get notified of special deals, local events and get more information. It doesn't matter what it is but you have to give them a reason to opt in and make it clear for them.

Capturing Leads to Build Your List

This is a topic that needs to be covered in much more detail and it will be later in the book. First of all, I want to give a short overview and explain why it is so important for your website.

If you listen to marketers, you will hear a lot about their "list" but they don't always tell you what it means.

When prospects come to your website and read about you, they may be excited. That's great until they get distracted by something or need to get on with another part of their day. They do something other than booking, calling you or making a reservation request on your booking engine.

Chances are they'll not remember to go back or they'll forget where they were.

That hot prospect is gone forever. You have no way of reaching them and you can't market to them.

This is where your list is so useful. This is where you get that group of people who want to know more and want to hear from you. You get to contact those people who want to buy your product or try out your services.

There are a few email services that will help you do this, such as Constant Contact, Aweber, iContact and many more. Most are really easy to use and affordable.

It's best to use these services instead of trying to do it all from your own email account—could you imagine trying to send hundreds of emails from your own email? You'll soon find your account being closed down! These services are specifically designed for email lists and comply with all those annoying regulations surrounding email marketing.

These services allow you to set up your list, create an easy-to-use form and give you the code needed for your website to set it all up. You can create the page to offer a brochure, a newsletter, get announcements of special offers, enter a VIP awards club or contact you for information.

The subscribers simply put in their name and email address for the offer. It's best to have this box show up on every single page. People won't always fill it out when they see it initially but they may join after seeing it a few times. With their email addresses, you can contact them until they decide they've had enough.

Contact Information

Make sure the phone number for your business stands out. The header is the perfect spot! You don't want your visitors to have to look around for this information or for the business address if you want them to come and visit you!

Credibility

Your visitors are always going to wonder if you offer them everything they need. They don't want to waste time on a company with shady tactics, someone whose offers aren't clear or those who they've had bad offers with in the past.

You need credibility and you can do that with the following:

- Adding a picture of yourself or your team

- Adding group or association logos you are linked or belong to

- Reviews and testimonials from happy customers

- Logos of the companies that customers can pay by

- Add Videos of your rooms, property, location and people

- Add any awards and nominations that you have won.

Now that you have the fundaments about keywords and ranking, it's time to build your website or, if you already have one, to make sure that it has the right messaging and design strategy to get more direct bookings.

Web Strategy Process

Message Before Design

Too often, website are designed by graphic artists who do not have a clue about messaging and marketing. This is a big mistake. It is absolutely essential to have your marketing strategy dictate the design and not the other way around. So job number one is to know your market and know what you unique seling point is.

Your Customer Avatar

Know your customers and create in your mind who is the perfect customer is. That then becomes you Avatar. You may have several avatars and if so, you may need to think of having separate pages for each. That can come later as you develop your offsite marketing and link back to specific pages to close to convert those travellers and get direct bookings.

Hot Buttons

The next step is to really understand your customer's hot buttons. Now this is critical and very seldom done in hospitality. It requires deep thinking of the benefits you can deliver to very specific clients, and knowing what problem or objection they have. Finally you have to answer their key questions and if you do not do this, they simply go elsewhere. The number one question that travel shoppers ask is: what is the value and how does this room, apartment, villa, etc. compare to the other option within the destination or other similar destinations?

Got that? Benefits, Objections and Competition. These are three of the most significant hot buttons. You need to wordsmith these, add a power image and create 3 hot button on your website first page. These are your main calls to action, or activators.

Messaging Formula & Neuroscience

Scientific studies of the mind, brain stimulation and behaviour show that people tune out messages unless they are familiar, unusual or problematic. For a person to switch off the automatic Alpha mode and start to pay attention (Beta wave mode) the message must also be relevant or important.

Power Marketing Consultants use a specific tried and proven formula to build the most effective marketing message that actually trigger action. That is the formula for creating hot buttons.

As a book buyer you have FREE access to our Powermembers' area which includes detailed accounts of the messaging formula that will help you create effective hot buttons.
http://powermembers.allcastmarketing.com

Website Design Formula

We are living in a visual age. High impact visual messages that are relevant, important and provide needed information trigger the mind into "pay attention" Beta mode. Hot button trigger videos with a strong voiceover message, music and visuals are powerful influencers. Google's research has shown that travellers who have viewed a video are 60% more likely to book.

Every page of you website should have a video. Accommodation pages must have images. We will cover that later.

 Our design layout is simple – An image across the top of product pages (rooms, accommodation). Feature images can have a 2:1 aspect ratio (i.e. 1200 wide x 600 high for desktop).

Under the image display your video. Product pages should have 4 images of product features and link to a photogallery. All pages should be Responsive - that mean that the display, content, images and videos change to adjust to the user's device and screen.

You can see samples of design in the pages summary below.

The Pages Your Business Website Need

There are a set number of pages your business website will need and this was covered extensively in my previous book.

This chapter offers tourism examples and concentrate on what is winning in site navigation.

- The Home Page: 'Home' is a good term to use. Google likes to see a home page as it is natural and it's clear what it is about. At one time we were using keywords instead of "Home". Like: Exotic Oceanfront Resort", but it's better to build good content about the page in the page.

- The About Page: It's good to name the page About-Brand name, or About-Keyword2*

- Accommodations/Rooms/Product pages*

- Contact Page

- Photo gallery and videos

- Bookings/Reservations

- Articles page

- Feedback & Reviews

- Your Privacy Page

Add some of your special keywords to the page names. Keep your keywords descriptive and relevant to the content.

The Home Page

This is usually the first page visitors will see and it is one of the hardest to make perfect. You've got about three seconds to make your visitors decide that they want to read more and you're what they need. It's also going to be the page that Google is more likely to notice.

Notice how this page has a video at the top. Under that is the call to action (Booking Button) followed by the Hot buttons. In this case, the buttons are:

1. Dealing with the objection of having to deal with crowds. It's the main feature of the offer and the objection of the target client "independent-minded travellers" who want authentic and independent holidays.

2. Your own Spacious Private Resort Villa Home is stacked with words that are trigger benefits for the avatar.

3. Value & Competition. This leads to a page that talks about the value proposition and compares the resort to others.

The About Page

This is extremely important for credibility and establishing yourself. This shows your visitors how qualified you are and how you will deliver on promises made within the unique selling proposition. People want to be able to trust a business and this is the chance to convey that they can trust you. In hospitality, travellers like to see photos of the people who will be their hosts.

Notice the video. In this case, there is no top image. It's important to have images for product pages and not essential in information pages. On this site, all primary pages have a video.

Accommodation/Products Pages

Provide a general overview of the type of accommodation and show one room of each type.

This accommodation page presents each unit type and links to the individual unit pages. It is a good idea to help your guest choose between units – some of that can be enabled via the menus.

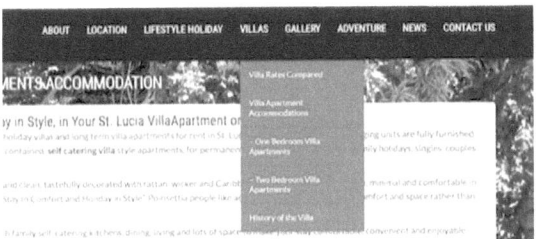

More advanced systems might include a picker like room with a garden and view, roof top terrace, etc. One can get very specific and look at character and colours of rooms. - In this website, guests are directed to the FAQ which includes a unit picker based on frequently asked question. The accommodation page image then links to the individual rooms, apartment or villas, each with an image followed by the video.

ONE BEDROOM VILLA 1 ROOFTOP TERRACE OCEAN VIEW

Villa 1 is up a short set of stairs that take you to the highest point at Poinsettia Apartments & Villas resort.

It's a good idea to have each room or unit integrated with your booking engine so you only need to maintain one set of amenities, photos and descriptions.

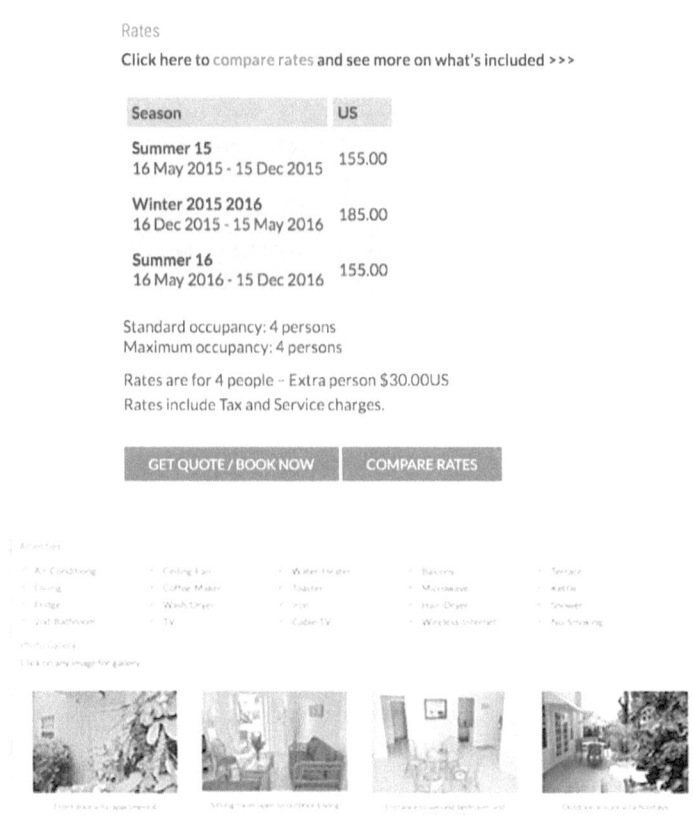

Rates

Notice that the rates and booking option are included right on the unit page. A while back, hotel websites tended to have rates on a separate page, but we have found that rates by themselves don't sell rooms.

A trend now is not to have rates on your pages at all, but have them show only when guests choose to check availability and book. I don't care for this. I find it annoying not to see the rate easily and make comparisons between different rooms and properties.

My preference is to have rates under the room descriptions and photos and to make the info and images sell the room/ product.

Also spell out your services, amenities and features over several pages. Add restaurants, spas, pools, beaches and attractions, as well as pages for rooms and suites and all normal tourism products. This is the best chance to highlight special factors in the delivery of your services. Google will want to know what you do so will look at this page.

Images

Four images are usually the minimum required. If you are a hotel with rooms only use: - A shot from the door to the bed and window - A view from the window out to the door is popular perspective. - Add a detail like a bedside light, chair or desk. - Show the bathroom.

For apartments and villas use a bedroom, living, kitchen and a detail like garden or bathroom.

The images should link to the photo gallery for each page.

Photo galleries today are moving to slideshows and Lightbox. I don't like them and our tests have shown they do not work as well as the carousel (above). Pinterest uses the carousel because people like to see the select not just one at a time. It offers perspective and more information at a glance.

Contact Page

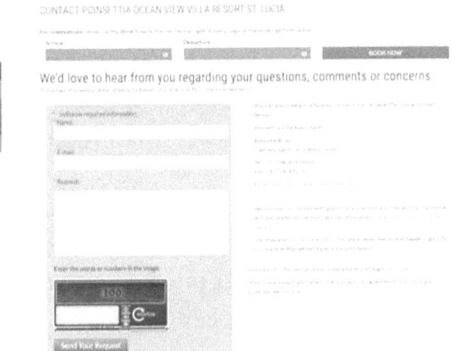

Just because your phone number is at the top of your website doesn't mean you don't need a contact page. This is really important as it includes the phone number, address and even a location map. Avoid adding your email address here unless you want to be swamped by people sending spam messages. Have a contact form instead for people to fill out.

Bookings/Reservations

Booking and reservation is really the ultimate purpose of your website. Make sure this is easy to find. Many websites have it as a highlighted "BOOK NOW" button. It's a good idea to have a similar button along with your rooms and descriptions, so that as someone reviews the description, they can check its availability, any special offers, etc.

Website Bookings and the tactics used to entice guests to book are vital. It's a bit advanced for this book and will be covered in detail in the next two books in the series.

Even though you may have a booking widget on every page, it's a good idea to also have a reservations page. This is where you can give travellers other options like book by email, ask a quest, and see answers to Frequently Asked Questions.

Most importantly, tell them why booking direct is the best option and show them your best rate guarantee. It is a sales page so don't list your boiler plate terms, instead explain them in terms of benefits and advantages, like (maybe) you only charge the credit card when they arrive.

If you have your own booking engine it will offer more features and benefits, such as; calculating the total cost of your holiday and, of course, it always gives you the best rate and special offers for the time of your booking. More about this in the next books.

Privacy Policy, Terms and Disclaimers

Privacy is required anytime you get personal information from a prospect. The Privacy Policy should be visible on all places that guests subscribe to bookings, services and to contact you. It's important to never reuse their information or to share it with anyone without the guest's consent. If you are working with a travel agent or booking service you do need to show this. They too have their privacy policies and it's a good idea to be sure they are adequate. Travellers understand that tourism companies may involve agents and 3rd party handlers but it is your responsibility to make sure that they too have privacy policies that protect the traveller. In some cases, tourism companies include statements about how the information may be used, as in the example below.

Your Information may be used to:
Mail brochures (if requested)
Email you an itinerary
Plan and purchase travel

Send notifications or communications
Respond to your questions or suggestions
Improve the quality of your visit to our site
Connect you with a destination specialist if required.

Articles Page (blog)

This is more of a blog but too many people get the wrong idea of that word. This isn't the type of blog that tells people personal stories about you. It's a way to publish on a regular basis, show your credibility and build engagement with your customers.

Your blog is the best way to keep your site current and keep adding content that search engines will index. It's a way to expand and reinforce your keywords. It can be a magnet for Google to send you more traffic. We cover this in detail in the chapter "Blogging For Travel".

Feedback & Reviews

Getting 5 star reviews is one of the most important ways you can create trust. Did you know that well over 90% of shoppers now read reviews before they purchase? Online Reviews are the digital equivalent of word of mouth advertising. In fact it is far more effective as it reaches a far greater audience.

That being said, it is imperative that you have a solid strategy in place to get 5 star reviews and to publish them strategically all over the internet. We will go into more detail on syndicating your reviews in the next book on digital media, but you can begin to lay the foundation for this strategy right now while perfecting your website presence. We will cover that in a following chapter called "Feedback & Reviews".

Reputation marketing as part of your branding will also be featured in the following series. But before we get carried away with fun marketing systems we need to be sure that our pages, site structure and navigation is optimised to provide a good user experience and is easily understood by Googles and the search engines.

Site optimisation, navigation and linking is vital. It is also where many websites fail.

Site Navigation and Linking

Your website is the place where you provide information to visitors that will persuade them to book with you. It should be designed in a way that leads people to make a commitment, get into a continuity program and book. Think of it as a spider's web. You lead people into pages, they apply for useful information, bookmark your site, sign on for services or book now.

Like a spider's web, your site will have catchment pages (also referred to as landing pages) with links to action pages.

The basic structure of the pages we have suggested are the main pillars of the site – all leading to making a reservation or responding to a call to action. The links to the call to action and between pages are important and the text in the links (link text) is vital.

You want to use your main keyword in links as much as possible. But with the recent changes by Google you cannot overdo the use of keywords within your site or to it.

Consider: you want to take viewers from the home page to a page where the keyword is "family holiday". Text on your home page will talk about a family holiday and link to a special page on family holiday options. Your family holidays page may offer special incentives to book a package NOW. It is a lead page that can become a landing page that other sites will pick up and link to (see more on this in Linking for Authority).

Not long ago we might have created this page and named it "family-holidays", then linked several pages to it all with the anchor text "family holidays".

That is now a NO-NO. It's what search engines now call unnatural and over-optimised.

Do Not Over-Optimise

People building links for themselves and linking to other site don't always optimise the anchor text in this way. They use alternative words like "holidays for all ages", "a great place for children", "your vacation" and other synonyms. They use non-optimised words like "click here", the brand name and the URL.

To be safe, use your main keyword in anchor about 1% of the time and never more than 5% if you have very balanced SEO. If your site domain name is an Exact Match Domain (EMD) or you are linking to a page with the keyword in its name, use only a single optimized link.

The rest of your links may be split equally between associate keywords, synonyms and semantic words, general categories and variations, and miscellaneous words like "get details" and "click here".

All of this is part of creating good SEO that will allow your site to get top ranking for related searches.

Silos

For the more extensive sites with lots of additional pages on amenities and holiday experiences, the typical site will have a hierarchical navigation. That is a set of menus at the top linking down to several pages under each menu. It has become the standard but it is not in fact the way that search looks at pages or even a good way to organise data. It is category-driven rather that sales-focused.

The new idea is to focus on one main keyword on a page and add up to 4 secondary words that are related to it and important to your business. Those 4 words then become 4 new pages which in turn may have 4 related words and pages associated.

We call this a 'silo structure' and it's hot right now because search engines rank well-organised information like silos well. In all cases the content needs to be high quality and deep. Don't setup tiny pages, as bigger is better. Google now favours pages that have over 800 words of quality content. Matt Cutts, head of Search Strategy at Google is on record as saying that for websites, some smaller pages are normal and expected. Travelers want the facts and most will get put off by too much detail, so try to organise content in logical blocks for them. Like all things, balance is needed and a hotel website should have long pages or blogs supported by a silo structure of related information.

So let's take an example: You have a page about *YourDestination* Holidays. Let's say that the 4 most relative and important words for you are: Family Holidays, Romantic Holidays, Adventure and Heritage. That is pretty typical for a tourism destination or a hotel.

What's not at all typical is that instead of having this as a drop down menu, you create a new top menu for your holidays page with these 4 items as the navigation. This new menu replaced the standard top menu which can still be reached via the home page. Now you need to have these secondary words included in the content of your main holiday page with a bit of information about each.

Each of the four pages link to the holiday page and to the previous page in the silo. The power of this silo structure is that the pages are very focused and highly targeted. The links are concentrated to pages that echo the focus entirely.

It also allows us to create more powerful sales funnels (see separate chapter) and it makes the information much more cohesive to search engines and data analysis. It does require considerable thought in planning your pages and navigation as you dive deeper into the data and try to understand the buyer's needs at every point.

For example: A family traveling (one of the 4 secondary keywords) has specific interested like kids programs, facilities for elders, baby sitting, etc. Likewise those on romantic vacations have different interests such as wedding, honeymoons, privacy, intimate settings and romantic things to do. You can see how very specific it can become and how information can expand as you dig down and explore the relationships.

The trick in building the silo is to keep the links focused within the silo and, unlike the traditional approach, not to link everything to everything. The silo feeds links back to its top page, carrying more weight and authority by restricting its focus back to the top. At the same time it helps travellers get very specific information without too much clutter and distraction.

It's a bit of an advanced subject but ask your webmaster about silo pages. It may not apply to your site but if it does, it can make a world of difference to your success.

You can build silos using your pages and your blog. Look at your content and you will find many areas that could be expanded. You might choose to expand it by adding another page but it is quicker just to add a blog. From the point of view of building the linking structure, a blog will do just as well.

For example, a key phrase and tag line that is repeated on the Poinsettia site is, "Stay in comfort and holiday in style".

It became so important in messaging, advertising and in explaining the unique selling point of the brand that a sperate video was made. The new video blog created the silo structure for the set of keywords. In the future more will be done to enhance the silo by adding relevant blogs. Each blog will link to the previous blog in the silo, creating a chain link back to the video page.

In this sense blogs are important, not only in broadcasting news but also in building an internal linking structure that will help you promote your site and its key pages.

We look at blogging in the next chapter.

Blogging for Travel

We often get a bit confused in talking about blogs. There are blogs you write on your own site and blogs or articles you post on the net, on other people's blogs and on article sites, online magazines, document sites and travel sites. The latter is off-site content marketing which is an important way to get links back to your site and publish your brand over the internet. That's covered in the next book.

This chapter is about blogging or writing stories and articles on your own site. It's a great way to add current content, to engage, to create continuity - a reason to return and help visitors. It also helps your site get indexed on search engines.

A blog can be about any number of ideas and topics. It can be news about your destination, festivals and events, guests' stories, staff stories and opinions, recipes from your chef and upgrades to your property, to mention just a few. Of course, your own story will make a great topic as people like to know who their host is what motivated you.

When writing a blog, remember that your blog is a place to interact and encourage guests to interact. Ask guests what they want to hear or talk about.

Polling software like: SurveyMonkey.com or GravityForms. com can help you streamline this process and analyze results.

Your blog is also a way to announce new services, pages, videos and technology that you add to your site, as well as hotel and tourism services and facilities added or upgraded.

How Much Work Is Involved?

Blogs are very similar to articles, which we cover in the next book. The difference is that they are more enjoyable to write. There's no need to follow the editorial guidelines of article directions—again, coming up. You can speak as you are talking and write about anything. It's possible to be opinionated, controversial and even promotional. As long as you cover your topic, it's fine.

You do need to remember your keyword strategy and make your heading snappy and interesting.

Here are a few pointers on writing blogs:

- Posts are generally about 500 words but can be any length. Even 300 words will work if the content is rich and enhanced with unique video and images. Longer blogs of high quality are more likely to rank on the first page of search results.

- Compelling titles are a must to play on the curiosity of your readers

Building & Marketing 5 Star Reviews

We don't recommend sending visitors directly off to TripAdvisor and other review sites on your prime pages. At least, not on top of every page, as many sites do. It is good to say "Recommended by TripAdvisor" but there is no need to link it everywhere.

TripAdvisor and other review services are vital and you need to work with them strategically, but remember that they are selling your competition. They often may list inappropriate choices appearing just under your property as good alternatives.

This was happening a lot. In the case of one villa resort, which was clearly mid range and excellent value at about 200$ per night for a villa for 4, TripAdvisor showed as an alternative a 90$ a night motel-style property that was in no way the villa's equivalent.

Travellers think that TA is recommending alternatives as an equivalent accommodation, and that brings down the perceived value. It can happen in reverse, with is great but you can't take that chance.

Visitors to your website are gold. You need to keep them on your site with whatever service they want for as long as possible.

That's why having a strategic review and feedback page is a must. This can all be automated with the right software. You will find several options if you do a search for "reputation management" or "holiday hotel review systems".

What you need is a system that will gather the reviews and repackage the review as a video, graphic and summary so that it can be displayed on your site.

TrustYou is perhaps one of the more established reputation management firms in the travel business and it does an excellent job. There are several alternatives and some of the newer technology offers additional features.

We have our own solution that has a built-in review marketing package. It is integrated with hotel websites so that guests can see 5 star reviews and leave reviews and comments of their own.

It semi-automates the creation of video reviews which are posted to the hotel website and the HolidayHotel.reviews marketing channel, along with Google and top media sites.

You can see this on the Poinsettia website at PoinsettiaVillas.com/feedback-reviews.

Reviews are an important part of a full reputation marketing system. We will be discussing that in more detail in the next series.

It is important to have a strategy to display the views appropriately on your site, get people to visit, read the reviews and to review your property.

Your website feedback option and review button makes it easier for guests to add a review with a single click.

13
Five Star Reviews
Found Around The Web
★ ★ ★ ★ ★

The button should allow guests to add a review, which can then be posted to your media centre, where you approve it for distribution.

The approved reviews are posted to your social media sites like LinkedIn, Facebook and image sites like Pinterest. The review is packaged in visual form suitable for each channel which gets more likes and views than a standard text post that you may do yourself.

These systems don't post the reviews to your TripAdvisor account, as your guest has to be signed in to do that. They do help streamline the process and will optionally send out email reminders and nicely worded requests on your behalf.

Getting guests to post reviews on TripAdvisor requires a constant attention to service and reminding them how important it is to you that they review and share their experience.

Use the TripAdvisor cards and collateral in rooms and around your property. You can also give TA the email of your guests when they leave and they will follow up for you. Of course it may not be all that they do with the email you give them, but if it helps get you reviews, it is worth the trade-off.

Lastly, remember that TA is not the only option. You want reviews on as many places as possible. This requires a proper emailing sequence and promotional campaign to remind guests and make it easier to leave reviews. These systems are included in most review and reputation marketing systems.

Your review management and reputation marketing will also give you cards and trade-show brochures, flyers and table tents, etc., that will help people find your website reviews and feedback page.

Video Enhanced Reviews

Several hotels are using video to repackage and syndicate reviews. Using professional voiceovers and a good script, along with images of your property, add empathy and personality to the review. It is an effective strategy and works well for small or large hotels, as well as activity providers, restaurants and anyone who has reviews. As a book buyer we invite you to try it for free. http://try.holidayhotelreviews.biz

Videos are very big in travel now. Travellers want to see images of the resort and destination, so it makes absolute sense to use video.

Remember how the "Power Marketing Web Strategy Process" of Chapter 5 advocates a video on every page of your website, each building on the hot button motivators? Well, these two strategies are so important today that I am going to take a closer look at them with you.

Let's do that now.

Hot Buttons & Videos

First, a Hot Button is not a feature or benefit. I recently added a blog on "The Death of Features and Benefits" - see http://markhat.com/ACKvi. To understand Hot Button you have to know the persona of your guests. Being on the beach might be of benefit to some but not to all. And for those that it is, it not the differentiator. It does not tell the story that will resonate the most.

For the New York stockbroker, being on the beach may very well be of benefit to him as he wants to fall into the water and soak away the stress. The Hot Button is "Soak Away the Stress", and being on the beach makes that a real possibility. We need to ask the question: so what? For the stressed out stockbroker, it is so he can jump into the dazzling clear Caribbean waters and "soak away the stress".

Marketing travel is all about selling the vision and the dream. Features and Benefits are for the text books, not the imagination. They alone do not tell stories or motivate buyers. So we have to ask ourselves: what is our Hot Button?

This book title is not a Hot Button. "Marketing Hotels and Tourism Online" is, in fact, rather academic. It is not obviously problematic, unusual or familiar, as we discussed in "Perfect your Presence". It is relevant and important to the viewer but it's not going to grab attention in a world full of books about the same thing.

My Mastermind Group agreed and suggested I change it for the title of the last book:

Are OTAs Eating your Apples? Or more directly **How to Prevent the OTAs from eating your apples**.

Now that is a Hot Button. It features a problem that is important to hoteliers and it is unusual wording: "OTAs Eating Apples?". It's familiar, as we all know apples and, if you remember from the preface, there is much symbology in the Apple. It a good Hot Button.

However, I did not want to use it for the entire series and it is not the feature of the first book. We don't get to OTAs until Book 3, and we need to work through Books 2 and 3 to get to the solution.

Book 1 (Website) and 2 (Digital Media) by themselves are not Hot Buttons but the titles, tag lines and topics are both good keywords and motivators. You bought the book; so they worked. Why? Because they refer to solving a problem which most hotel and tourism operators have. - not understanding what to do. So the academic title is somewhat appropriate. Maybe the Apple makes is seem easy. In messaging, we are often dealing with symbols.

So, how do we apply that to hotel videos? It's not hard - just find the big problems that travellers have and create a video for each. Some video can be just visual explanations of your why and what. Here are some examples:

Competition

Most travellers will want to know about the competition. Why not show them your value compared to other?

Fear

They may be afraid of going to a destination far away. A video on safety explaining the location and neighbourhood would help.

Weather

Weather is always an issue for travellers. Think about doing a spokesperson video showing sunny days and talking about the seasons, temperature and what to wear. Say engaging things like: "It gets a little chilly in the evenings and locals often put on a jumper to sit out in the evening breeze. But you would not need that coming from Canada".

Personality

Videos are personal so don't be afraid of showing who you are; it is what connects. Adding personal details like "You wil not need a jumper coming from Canada", makes it highly relevant. We will talk more about your guests persona and behaviour responsive websites later.

Place & Space

How much space is in my room? What's the view like? You do video for each room type and lots of views, garden, even the birds - all great subjects. Do a video on your mission - your "WHY" - and get on camera.

Location

Travellers find it hard to judge a neighbourhood from maps and brochures. A video of local places, local attractions, the places next door, your favourite nearby restaurant and how easy it is to get to places they may want to see is important.

10x10 Strategy

Mike Keonigs, who was one of the early pioneers in video marketing and the creator of Traffic Geyser, which helped syndicate video all over the web, has a video making principle which he call the 10x10.

That is, do a video for the 10 Frequently Asked Questions (FAQs,, like those above) and the 10 "Should Ask" questions (SAQs).

SAQs are sort of what you should know but don't know how to ask. It's what you might tell a really good friend about your place and the competition. It's what you might tell them to ask about the competition.

"Is there an A La Carte selection in an all-inclusive, or is it always buffet?" It's a way to point out your differentiation.

The SAQ gets to the heart of what the service should be. Some all-inclusives have great food and good variety but some are tired of buffets with overcooked vegetables. So the real differentiation between the good and not-so good is: "are all-inclusive meals placed in steamers and under hot lights with waterlogged vegetables and dried-out chicken?" I think you get the picture.

Well, maybe not!

You may not want to word it in just that way. It's rather negative and hostile, but I think you know what I mean. SAQs are the provocateurs and your video is showing you do it right, right?

Short Snappy Videos

The video of the FAQs & SAQs can be very short and they are usually 1 minute or less. You can make them longer but 2 to 3 minuets is about all the attention you can expect, so have a lot of small videos rather than few long ones.

The principles of video production will vary a bit, but as a rule of thumb, they are: problem, solution, benefit and proof. That is a good formula. In some cases, it's just a visual but try to have a voiceover.

Voiceover

A voice adds personality, credibility, emotion and intimacy. It certainly helps with the story and description. More importantly, it helps with search engines and Google. Why? Because they transcribe the script and scan the keywords. Also, they are looking for effort and rich content. An authentic voice on video adds greatly to the creditability.

Autoplay

Have you noticed how Facebook has shot up in the ranks with its video now competing with YouTube for top spot? Well, a lot of that has to do with autoplay. They turn the sound off but the movement alone gets people's attention and they click. Using autoplay with sound muted is a good strategy for videos on your site.

Autoplay does not work on Mobile at this time, so you can't rely on it to display your message on that platform.

Is it Mobile Friendly?

In our case study for Poinsettia,we have an autoplay video on the front page. It has the hot button messaging right in the video, but that does not work on mobile. So, for mobile we created a still image with the messaging below.

Mobile is a special case for everything, including video. It effects all your layout, technology and content. We will take a look at what's good to know about mobile in the next chapter.

FREE REPORT & CHECKLIST

As a Book Buyer you may access our Checklist on How to Optimise your YouTube Videos after you register at http://bonus.MarketingHotelsTourismonline.com

Make Your Site Mobile Friendly

Regardless of how great your website is and how well it Search Engine Optimised, you will fail if it's not mobile optimised.

People are looking for information and planning travel through their mobile devices. In fact, a growing number are booking via smartphones and tablets. In our case we see many sites with 50% of users accessing our main travel sites, like Barbados.org, by a mobile device.

According to Expedia, 20% of consumers book their travel on mobile (via mobile apps or a mobile website) and a majority use mobile devices to research and plan their travel. See latest stats at:

http://marketinghotelsandtourism.com/?s=mobile

By the time you read this book, the number of travellers using a mobile, smartphone or tablet to search the Internet will probably be more that those using traditional laptop and desktop computers to search. So, you need to make sure your website is accessible for these customers right now.

It is also something you need to do to get listed or maintain your listing on Page 1 of search results. Google made that mandatory late in 2015 when they announced that they were giving preference to mobile friendly sites.

Travellers started using their smartphones and tablets to research and plan travel from wherever they were and whenever they had a moment to spare. Think about it. When you're travelling, running errands, waiting for appointments or the kids, you'll search for products and services with your mobile device. You don't wait until you get home, do you? Most don't if they have web-enabled devices and smartphones. It's the same for travel, except the planning stage is longer and more detailed so travellers are even more inclined to u check out holiday options on the go.

More and more travel shoppers are also booking on line. eMarketing predicts that in 2016 over 50% of online travellers will book from their mobile device.

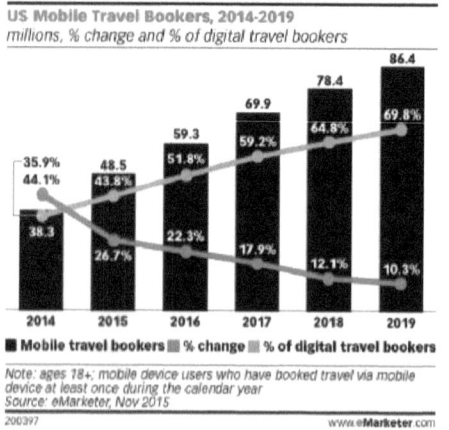

US Mobile Travel Bookers, 2014-2019
millions, % change and % of digital travel bookers

Note: ages 18+; mobile device users who have booked travel via mobile device at least once during the calendar year
Source: eMarketer, Nov 2015

200397   www.eMarketer.com

That is ahead of previous estimates. In 2014 Phocuswright estimated that 20% of all online booking would be by mobile in 2015. Thomsons UK says that 25% of all their online bookings are coming from mobile devices. At Expedia it is 20% and growing. Facebook's mobile logins account for 60% of all visits and at Barbados.org, mobile is now over 50% of all traffic. Latest articles and stats search for 'mobile bookings on:

http://marketinghotelsandtourism.com/?s=mobile+booking

This is great for those who do have mobile-friendly websites. It's important that they load quickly and people can navigate quickly on the small touch screen devices. Think about how you feel when you get a website that doesn't load as fast as you want—you move on, right? What do you do when a website is complicated or difficult to navigate around? You move on and customers will do the same with you. Your bounce rate increases because of that.

But you can't just settle for easy navigation. Your website needs to offer all the information that the original website would, but in a more concise way. People don't want to read through lots of details on their mobile device. They want to see the right information quickly. You want to grab their attention so they stay there and decide that your business offers everything they need.

Responsive Web Design (RWD)

This is where it gets technical, but it's important if you want to make the most of your website. You can choose to either build a separate mobile website or create a single site which configures the information and display based on which device your customer is using.

This second approach is known as Responsive Web Design (RWD) and is the current trend. Using RWD means that you only have one site (and one set of information) to keep up to date. It is also the method recommended by Google for serving up mobile content.

If you only want to offer a small amount of very action-centered content to your mobile users, then a separate mobile site may be used instead of RWD. But remember, more and more mobile users are expecting a full-featured experience, not a dumbed-down one with limited content.

Multi-Screen-Shift

Today, online shoppers often begin tasks on Smartphones and later go to their laptop or desktop computers to adjust, fine-tune and complete the task. A 'Google Think Insights' study suggests that up to 90% of people used multiple devices to accomplish a goal.

To meet these expectations, your content must adapt to any and all screens and the user experience must be coordinated across all devices. Really, the only way to achieve this is with a Responsive Web Design. For example, a traveller may select options on one device and add them to a wish list. He or she will want the choices to be available again on the next device used. Using customer profiles, you can save these choices across multiple devices. RWD presents the information to the traveller in a consistent, yet optimised, manner across all their devices.

It doesn't matter who built the website or how it was done; you can still check the performance from your own device. You could also ask friends, employees and family to check the performance for you so you can check a range of devices.

Applications (Apps)

You do not need to build your mobile website as an app. Apps are great for OTAs and services that offer a lot more than site browsing. Apps are great for services like early check in, fast check out, billing, room key, loyalty programs, concierge and room services. For online information, reservations and booking, your provider should offer a mobile version - that's all you need. If you have a custom-built booking engine, make sure it is mobile responsive.

The point is that users are not likely to download apps for all hotels they consider when planning a holiday. They may download an app from suppliers that they have loyalty programs with, but to check rates and availability at a hotel, they prefer to browse.

Apps are however more likely to be downloaded if they cover many hotels and offer search and filtering. Travel shoppers are more likely to download an app from Booking.com and other OTAs. Of course, all this may change: Google has just started indexing apps and streaming the information to browsers.

http://marketinghotelsandtourism.com/?p=3909

Other Options

Early in 2016 Google decided that RWD was often poorly implemented and not offering the best experience for mobile users. Many web shops just do not do a rigerous job of resizing images and changing content to adapt to the many different devices. It's easy to take short cuts and many hotel managers and tourism markers will never know the difference. Google, of course, does and so do travellers.

Big G has decided it's time for a new mobile markup language that forces designers to minimize for mobile. It is an idea that is similar to the first .mobi site tools. We will create a report on this new AMP language (Accelerated Mobile Pages) and add details to the book buyer bonus. So far we can't see great value in not doing RWD, if you do it right, but their are trade-offs. One area of concern is that it is another Google tool that hooks us in to further dependence and exposes our copyright content, which they don't mind borrowing for their growing list of travel products.

To Sum Up

Whatever you do, be sure that all you do - from booking to blogging - will work well on mobile. Over 90% of US adults own a mobile phone and as we noted previously, more and more travellers are using mobile devices to plan and book travel. Be sure that all parts of your website - from your images, your video and blogs - will work on whatever device travellers are using.

NEXT BOOK >> DIGITAL MEDIA

So, now that you know how to make your website effective, powerful and mobile ready — and you know a good bit on how to get Google to love your site — In the next book, DIGITAL MEDIA, we look at your offsite marketing and how to build your digital network and reputation to get found and get booked. It covers building your footprint, getting on the map, mobile marketing, social media, sales funnel, staying on top, guide to the future, offsite evaluation tools.

YOUR BOOK BUYERS BONUS

Our team of developers at AXSES AllCast Power Marketing have created a FREE checklist for **mobile web design and marketing**.

You may also get the FREE checklist of how to **Optimise your videos on YouTube** plus lost more.

As registered book buyer member I will personally invite you to **the Pre-launch offer of the next book**.

Get these and **other bonuses, tips and video tutorials** on the following page

Thank You for Reading

Thank You for Reading My Book

I would love your feedback. If you can spare a moment please add a short comment on the Amazon review pages.

Get Your Bonuses at:

http://Bonus.MarketingHotelsTourismOnline.com

1. **Pre-launch Offer** on Next Book. Expected @ 99c

2. FREE Checklist of how to **Optimise YouTube Videos**

3. Free **Mobile Website CheckList**

4. Free **Tips & Video Tutorials**

ALSO we invite you to take advantage of our **Special Offer for book buyers**

i. FREE Trial offer on **Reputation Marketing**. Includes Free video, syndication and website integration

ii. Special Offer on AllCast Power Marketing **Website Evaluation and leverage report**

Contact me:

http://Buyers.MarketingHotelsTourismOnline.com

Facebook.ianrclayton.com | Google.ianrclayton.com | twitter.ianrclayton.com |

This book on Amazon:

http://www.amazon.com/Marketing-Hotels-Tourism-Online-Website-ebook/dp/B0196D0OJS/

Glossary

Above the Fold
Just like on a newspaper at a newsstand, you can only see part without flipping the paper over. On a website, this is the part that's visible without scrolling.

Affiliate
Someone who promotes your products and services and gets paid based on results.

Algorithm
How search engines create a list of search results based on the search term. Algorithms change regularly to yield better search results.

ALT Text
Coding that tells the search engines about images and other non-textual elements that can't be displayed.

Analytics
Graphs and charts that provide information on your website's traffic and the source and behavior of your site's visitors.

Anchor Text
Words, phrases, or images that are 'clickable'. When you click, you are taken to another part of the website or elsewhere on the Internet.

B2B
Business to Business marketing

B2C
Business to Consumer marketing

Backlinks
Links coming into your website from another place online. Backlinks help with SEO because some algorithms calculate the quantity and quality of backlinks when determining search engine result ranking.

Below the Fold
Any part of a webpage you have to scroll down to see.

Black Hat SEO
Search engine optimization that uses unethical methods.

Blog
An online journal or article page that is updated frequently, usually allows comments.

Bots
Short for the robots (also called spiders) that scan the Internet for search engines.

Bounce
When a visitor reaches your website and leaves it quickly without visiting any other pages on your site.

Bounce Rate
The percentage of your site visitors that bounce.

Browser
An application that enables you to access and navigate the Internet.

Code
Information written in any of several computer languages.

Competing Pages
The total of webpages that are focused on a single keyword.

Conversion Rate
The percentage of how many clicks to your site generate a sale or a lead.

Crawl
An automated process where search engine algorithms gather information about websites.

Deep Linking
Linking to a page on your website other than your Home Page.

Description Tag
An HTML (code) tag that provides a description of the page for search engine listings.

Directory
An index of websites, usually created by human editors. Usually require editorial approval for inclusion.

Directory Optimization
Writing a directory submission in a way that makes it most relevant for search engines to increase the chances of the site coming up when someone searches with your keywords.

Domain
A text Internet address ending in a dot and three letters (i.e. .com, .net, .org, etc.). In countries outside the U.S. domain names end with a two letter country code.

Duplicate Content
Webpages that have the same content – can be on a single website or on different websites.

Ecommerce
Buying and selling products and services online.

Exact Match Domains (EMD)
Urls with exactly match the keywords. This is a filter Google launched in September 2012 to prevent poor quality sites from ranking well simply because they had words that match search terms in their domain names.

Flame
Comments or messages posted with the intention of being rude or abusive.

Geo Targeting
Adding geographical information to marketing campaigns to make the marketing pieces more likely to appear to searchers in that location.

Google Dance
Each time Google changes its algorithms, Internet marketers scramble to understand the impact of that change and then make any adjustments needed to their online marketing.

Google Sandbox
For various reasons – from having a brand new site to employing Black Hat SEO tactics – sometimes Google essentially shuns a website, and it basically disappears from search engine results.

Google Smack
Getting your site put into the Google Sandbox.

Googlebot
See bot.

Googles Hummingbird
Hummingbird is Googles search update of September 2013. It focuses on the whole query and evaluates the meaning rather than looking at particular words. The goal is that pages matching the meaning do better than pages matching just a few words.

Googles Panda
Google's search update that de-listed low quality, spammy and duplicate content.

Google's Penguin
Google search update aimed at over optimized links.

Hidden Text
Text added to a webpage that is the same color as the page's background, making it invisible to humans. Search engines can read the text. This is a Black Hat SEO tactic.

Home Page
The main page of a website, its main point of entry.

Hyperlink
A bit of text or an image you can click on a webpage that takes you somewhere else, either on that page or to another page or another website.

Inbound Link
Any link that comes into your site from another website.

Keyword
What someone types in when they search for information online. Can be a single word or a phrase.

Keyword Density
How many times a keyword appears on a page for every 100 words.

Keyword Research
Research done to determine how people are searching online for the information, products, and services you offer.

Keyword Stuffing (or Keyword Spam)
Trying to include too many repetitions of a keyword in an article or website content in an effort to trick search

engines into giving higher importance to the website. This is a Black Hat SEO tactic.

Keywords Tag

A list of relevant keywords for a website, entered into the coding of the site. Early on, the search engines paid attention to the keywords tag – now most ignore it completely, as its abuse was an easy Black Hat SEO tactic.

Landing Page

The page on a website where you land after clicking through a link on another website – either from an affiliate's page, an article, press release, or video. It is designed to get a visitor to take action.

Link Building

An SEO practice of building links back to your website. This has the goal of boosting a website's traffic and improving its ranking in the search engines. Links can be created with articles, press releases, videos, blog posts, etc.

Link Checker

An automated tool that helps identify broken hyperlinks on a website.

Link Popularity

How many sites link to your site, and how well-respected by the search engines those sites are.

List
An email marketing list comprised of site visitors who provided their name and email address, willingly giving you permission to market to and contact them.

Long Tail
Keyword phrases 2-5 words long. They get fewer searchers, but they are more targeted and often yield better conversion rates.

Manual Submission
Building backlinks by hand rather than by using an automated tool.

Meta Tags
Bits of code that provide information to search engines about a website. They include Title Tags, Description Tags and Keyword Tags.

Mobile Accelerated Pages
A set of standards developed by Google and Twitter designed for pure readability and speed, It is a striped down version of HTML for mobile websites.

Navigation
How you move from page to page in a website.

Organic Search Listings
Listings in a search engine that are not sponsored, or purchased, as an advertisement.

Outbound Link
A link that leads to a website that's not your site.

Page Rank
Search engines use algorithms to determine the relevance of a website, then list them in order of relevance.

Podcasts
Audios and videos that can be distributed online, downloaded, and played on a personal computer or mobile device.

PPC (Pay Per Click)
Paid placement in a search engine. Your ads only show up when someone enters the keywords you bid on for your ad. You only pay when someone clicks your ad.

Reciprocal Links
Links exchanged between website owners.

RSS (Real Simple Syndication)
A way to syndicate your blog content online so it reaches subscribers automatically every time you update the content.

Search Engine
A program that scours the Internet in the attempt to match searches and web pages.

SEO (Search Engine Optimisation)

Working on a website to make sure it is found easily by people using targeted keywords to search for information, products, and services online.

Search Engine Submission

Submitting URLs to search engines to make the engine aware of their existence.

SERP (Search Engine Results Page)

The results you see after doing a search in a search engine. The SERP includes sponsored ads and organic search listings in a list.

Social Media

Various websites that feature user-contributed content, including social networking sites, forums, blogs, video sharing sites, and more.

Title Tag

An HTML tag coded to create the text that shows up in the top line of a browser when you visit a website. Also used by search engines to help them provide relevant search results.

Top Ten

The top ten websites appearing in the organic search listings on a SERP.

Unique Visitor

An actual, real visitor to your website. Unique visitor stats don't include bots or repeat visitors, so this is an important statistic to measure.

URL

The Internet location of a webpage. Follows the format http://www.domain.com.

Web Directory

An organized, categorized listing of websites, sometimes centered on a specific topic.

About the Author

Ian R. Clayton is the author of "How to build Your Business Online". His insights, articles, blogs and videos on technology, media, the environment and travel have been featured across the Internet, in magazines and in major news media, including the New York Times and the Financial Times of Canada.

As CEO of AXSES, Ian and his team work hands-on with hospitality and tourism professionals to build game-changing applications, marketing campaigns and sales systems for hotels and tourism companies of all sizes.

The team recently lunched a new website which is dedicated to helping hotel and tourism professionals master online marketing to grow their businesses.

TourismMarketingMachines.com,

Their latest innovations:

VisualBookingsTechnology.com, has doubled the rate at which travellers visit hotel website in live installations. HolidayHotelReviews.biz is the latest venture. It brings visual animation and video to review marketing and reputation management.

Ian has also worked as a chef, a hotel general manager and the vice president of an international distribution company before starting his own company AXSES Inc, in 1984.

Ian lives in Canada and loves to travel as frequently as possible, especially to the Caribbean.

Books by Ian R Clayton

Published:

"**How to Build Your Business Online**"   A general look at much of the content in this book. This book was nominated for a small business award.

"**Marketing Hotels & Tourism Online**"   **WEBSITE** This is a 'Hotel & Tourism' version of the Build Your Business Online Series. It is more current of course and in addition to its focus on tourism and real life examples of hospitality marketing, it also covers new trends and the changes in search marketing.

Coming Soon:

DIGITAL MEDIA & TECHNOLOGY

"**Sales Tactics, Technology & Resources for Hospitality, Hotels and Tourism Marketing**" The third in the Build Your Business Online Series. It covers advanced and special marketing issues in building the hospitality, tourism and destination brand. It also devolves into the Sales Funnel in Travel and look at how we can **Building a Better Sales Funnel for Tourism**". When you look around at how business' sell, they use lead magnets, trip-wires and all sort of up-sell and down-sell techniques. They understand the mental triggers that lead to a sale and execute them well. I am not salesman, but ethical sales psychology is something we all need to understand. I think we have a lot of room to improve selling in travel. It is the face-to-face, personal and emotional part of marketing that deserves its own story.

Travel Stories

"Rogues in Paradise" A whimsical account of life in the islands. Meet the village personalities you will not find in your hotel.

Book Buyers Bonus

Don't forget to get your Free Bonuses at:

http://Bonus.MarketingHotelsTourismOnline.com

Instructions are on that page and it's very simple. The Bonuses may change, we will add more surprises, and all registered buyers will be advised.

Get Next eBook @99c

Book buyers who register for the BookBuyers bonus will be eligible for the pre-launch offer of the next book in the series. This is subject to terms by Amazon which may change at any time.

www.ingramcontent.com/pod-product-compliance
Lightning Source LLC
Chambersburg PA
CBHW021547200526
45163CB00016B/2800